# The Ship That Lived The Incredible Story of USS Phoenix and General Belgrano

By Hugh Ravenscroft

## Introduction: A Ship with Two Lives

Few warships in history can claim such a dramatic and unlikely arc of service as the cruiser that began life in the United States as USS *Phoenix* and ended it, four decades later, in the South Atlantic as ARA *General Belgrano*. To trace her journey is to walk a path through some of the most turbulent decades of the twentieth century, decades shaped by global war, Cold War rivalries, shifting alliances, and, finally, the bitter conflict between Britain and Argentina in the remote waters around the Falkland Islands. Hers was not simply the tale of a warship, but of the people who built her, commanded her, sailed her, and died upon her decks. She embodied the ambitions of two nations, carried the pride of two navies, and ultimately became a symbol of endurance, tragedy, and controversy.

The *Phoenix* was conceived in a world still reeling from the First World War, yet already preparing for another. During the interwar years, international treaties sought to limit the tonnage, armament, and deployment of warships in an attempt to prevent another ruinous naval arms race. The Washington Naval Treaty of 1922 and the London Naval Treaty of 1930 both imposed restrictions designed to keep naval competition within bounds, but such limitations encouraged as much evasion as compliance. Naval architects around the globe sought ways to squeeze maximum firepower and protection into the allowed displacement. The result was a generation of cruisers that tested the spirit, if not the letter, of the treaties.

The Brooklyn-class, to which *Phoenix* belonged, was the United States' direct response to Japanese warship construction in the 1930s. Japan had launched a series of heavily armed cruisers that outmatched anything in the American arsenal, forcing the U.S. Navy to act. The Brooklyn-class ships were designed to carry fifteen six-inch guns, far more than most cruisers of their day, and to provide both speed and endurance for Pacific operations. *Phoenix*, laid down in 1935 at the New York Shipbuilding Corporation's yards in Camden, New Jersey, was a product of that competitive environment. She was not a battleship, nor an aircraft carrier, but a swift and lethal ship designed to project American influence across the world's oceans.

By the time she joined the fleet in 1938, international tensions were worsening. Europe drifted towards war as Germany rearmed and Italy pursued an empire, while in Asia, Japan's aggression in China unsettled the Pacific. The United States remained officially neutral but increasingly aware that its own security could not be isolated from these global developments. For the officers and sailors assigned to *Phoenix*, peacetime service was filled with drills, exercises, and patrols that seemed routine but were, in reality, sharpening skills for the conflict to come.

Her moment arrived on the morning of 7 December 1941. Moored at Pearl Harbour, Hawaii, *Phoenix* lay near the battleships that symbolised American naval power. When the Japanese attack began, her crew scrambled to their stations as bombs fell and torpedoes tore open the mighty battleships nearby. The air filled with the roar of engines, the crack of anti-aircraft guns, and the screams of men thrown into the oily harbour waters. The *Phoenix*'s gunners fired back at the attackers with determination, though, like most American ships that day, they were taken by surprise. Unlike the battleships *Arizona*, *Oklahoma*, and *West Virginia*, however, the cruiser escaped severe damage. With her engines intact, she powered her way out to sea, one of the few ships to emerge from the devastation unscathed. For her crew, the attack transformed their world in a single morning. They had arrived in port as peace-time sailors; they steamed out into the Pacific as combatants in a global war.

From that day forward, *Phoenix* became part of the long, grinding campaign across the Pacific. She provided escort for convoys, supported amphibious landings, and engaged in surface actions against Japanese forces. Her gunners defended against relentless air raids, including kamikaze attacks in the war's final months. She was often in the thick of the fight, yet time and again she emerged with her hull intact, earning a reputation as a "lucky ship." Sailors are prone to superstition, and for the men of the *Phoenix*, their cruiser seemed touched by fortune. She was not invulnerable, but she endured where others perished.

The experiences of her crew mirrored those of thousands of Americans in the Pacific War. They lived in cramped quarters, endured long stretches of monotony punctuated by moments of terror, and formed bonds of camaraderie that only combat can forge. On board, men from across the United States—farm boys, city dwellers, factory workers—learned to live and fight together. They sweated in tropical heat, subsisted on Navy rations, and counted the days until they could see home again. For many, the *Phoenix* became more than a ship; she was their protector, their workplace, and their community afloat.

By 1945, the *Phoenix* had completed a remarkable journey. From the shock of Pearl Harbour, she had steamed through countless battles and operations, and when Japan finally surrendered, she was present at Tokyo Bay. To be there on 2 September 1945, when representatives of the Japanese Empire signed the documents of surrender aboard USS *Missouri*, was to witness the closing act of the greatest war in history. For the men of the *Phoenix*, it felt like vindication: they had survived the worst, and their ship had carried them safely through.

In the years that followed, the U.S. Navy rapidly downsized. With hundreds of new ships built during the war and the threat of demobilisation pressing, older vessels like the *Phoenix* were placed in reserve. She remained in American hands until 1951, when geopolitical realities once again reshaped her destiny. The Cold War was in full swing, and the United States sought to strengthen allies around the world. South America, often overlooked in global strategic discussions, was a region where Washington wanted to build goodwill and counterbalance Soviet influence. Transferring surplus ships to friendly governments was one way to do so.

Argentina, with its proud naval tradition and ambition to assert itself as a regional power, was eager to acquire modern warships. When the United States agreed to sell the *Phoenix* along with another cruiser, Argentina saw an opportunity to boost its fleet dramatically. The ship was renamed ARA *General Belgrano*, honouring Manuel Belgrano, a revered leader of Argentina's independence movement. The rechristening was more than a change of name; it was a rebirth. What had once been a symbol of American might became a vessel of Argentine pride.

Under the Argentine flag, the *Belgrano* was not simply a second-hand cruiser. She became a floating emblem of national prestige. She carried dignitaries, hosted naval cadets, and participated in exercises that showcased Argentina's ability to operate a serious blue-water fleet. For generations of Argentine sailors, she was a formative experience: a place to learn discipline, seamanship, and service to the nation. She represented a bridge between Argentina's colonial past and its aspirations for modern influence.

Yet the ship's second life was destined for tragedy. In 1982, Argentina invaded the Falkland Islands, claiming sovereignty over the territory long held by Britain. The decision sparked one of the most improbable wars of the twentieth century, fought thousands of miles from Europe in the stormy South Atlantic. Britain dispatched a naval task force to retake the islands, and the *Belgrano* was sent south to threaten the British fleet. On 2 May, she was struck by torpedoes fired from HMS *Conqueror*, a British nuclear-powered submarine. Within minutes, the cruiser that had survived Pearl Harbour and carried Argentine pride sank beneath the waves.

The loss of the *Belgrano* was catastrophic. Three hundred and twenty-three Argentine sailors perished—nearly half of the nation's total fatalities in the war. Survivors clung to lifeboats in freezing seas, awaiting rescue that took hours to arrive. For Argentina, the sinking became a national trauma, remembered as both a tragedy and a symbol of sacrifice. For Britain, it was a decisive military blow that removed a significant threat to its fleet. For the wider world, it sparked intense controversy. The *Belgrano* had been outside Britain's declared exclusion zone when attacked. Was the sinking justified as an act of war against an enemy cruiser, or was it an unnecessary escalation that cost hundreds of lives? The debate continues to this day, entangling military strategy with politics, morality, and memory.

The ship that lived twice thus became far more than steel and rivets. She was a witness to history's great upheavals: the surprise at Pearl Harbour, the triumph at Tokyo Bay, the aspirations of post-war Argentina, and the bitter conflict of the Falklands. She was a vessel of endurance and of tragedy, her story entwined with the lives of those who served on her decks. Her guns fired in anger under two flags, her decks bore the footsteps of two navies, and her final resting place lies in the cold waters of the South Atlantic, a war grave and a symbol.

This book tells her whole story—from conception to destruction, from triumph to loss, from one flag to another. Along the way, we will examine not just the ship herself but also the broader forces that shaped her fate: the industrial power of America, the pride of Argentina, and the shifting tides of geopolitics. We will meet the sailors and officers who called her home, learn how she was deployed, and consider how her legacy endures.

The *General Belgrano*'s tale is not only about naval history. It is about how nations remember, how they grieve, and how they project their aspirations upon great ships. She was, in many ways, the boat that lived twice. And through her story, we glimpse the human drama of the twentieth century itself—lived at sea, under fire, and beneath the banners of two nations.

## Chapter 1: Forged in Steel – Building USS *Phoenix*

The warship that would one day be known as ARA *General Belgrano* began her life not under an Argentine flag, nor in the stormy South Atlantic, but in an American shipyard along the banks of the Delaware River. In the mid-1930s, the New York Shipbuilding Corporation in Camden, New Jersey, was one of the busiest yards in the United States. Its cavernous slipways rang with the sounds of rivet hammers, welding torches, and the shouts of thousands of workers who, even before America formally entered the Second World War, were already shaping the steel that would carry the nation to conflict. Amid the industrial clamour and the lingering economic shadows of the Great Depression, the keel of a new light cruiser was laid down in 1935. She was to be named *Phoenix*, after the mythical bird that rises from the ashes, an apt name for a ship conceived in a world recovering from one great war and moving inexorably toward another.

### The World in Transition

The mid-1930s were a time of profound unease. Only two decades had passed since the First World War, and yet the fragile peace was already crumbling. In Europe, Adolf Hitler's Nazi regime was openly defying the Treaty of Versailles, rearming Germany at a breathtaking pace and reoccupying the Rhineland. Mussolini's Italy was expanding aggressively in Africa, while in Asia, Japan had invaded Manchuria and was grinding forward into China, seeking an empire that would dominate the Pacific.

Against this backdrop, the United States found itself in a difficult position. Scarred by the trauma of the First World War, many Americans still clung to isolationist ideals, believing the Atlantic and Pacific Oceans were sufficient shields against foreign conflict. Yet military planners could see the storm clouds gathering. The Washington and London Naval Treaties of the 1920s and early 1930s had sought to limit naval arms races, but these agreements were already fraying. Japan, in particular, was building heavily armed cruisers that threatened to outmatch anything the U.S. Navy could put to sea in the Pacific. Something had to be done.

The response was the Brooklyn-class of light cruisers, a new generation of ships designed to comply technically with treaty restrictions while offering maximum firepower and speed. They were warships crafted with both diplomacy and deterrence in mind—sleek, versatile, and bristling with guns. It was within this strategic calculation that the *Phoenix* took shape.

**The Brooklyn-Class**

The Brooklyn-class represented a significant leap forward in cruiser design. Their primary distinguishing feature was their main armament: fifteen six-inch guns, mounted in five triple turrets. This gave them more firepower than many contemporary heavy cruisers, even though treaty definitions kept them in the "light" category due to the calibre of their weapons.

In addition to their main battery, the Brooklyns carried secondary anti-aircraft guns and were designed with the speed to keep up with fast carrier task forces. Their propulsion systems could drive them at speeds exceeding thirty knots—crucial for both offensive and defensive operations. Armour protection, while not as heavy as on battleships, was robust enough to withstand hits from enemy cruisers and smaller ships.

The *Phoenix*, like her sister ships, measured over 600 feet in length and displaced around 9,700 tons when fully loaded. She was long and lean, her superstructure streamlined to reduce her silhouette against the horizon. Her dual funnels gave her a distinctive profile, one that would later be instantly recognisable in photographs from Pearl Harbour to Tokyo Bay.

## Building in Camden

The construction of the *Phoenix* at Camden was as much a human story as an industrial one. At the height of the Depression, shipyard contracts meant steady wages for thousands of families. Men in overalls trudged through the gates each morning, lunch pails in hand, to spend long hours riveting steel plates or threading electrical systems through narrow passageways. The noise of the yard was constant—a cacophony of steel being shaped into order, into something greater than its parts.

For many of the workers, the ship was not an abstraction of strategy or foreign policy. She was bread on the table, shoes for children, and security in an uncertain world. The pride of building a warship also carried a special resonance. These were not anonymous factories churning out products for anonymous markets. To work at Camden was to know that your hands were helping to build something that would sail the oceans under the Stars and Stripes, carrying the might of the United States Navy across the globe.

Women, too, played a role. Though their numbers would swell later during the Second World War, even in the 1930s, women were employed in clerical roles and as support staff in the shipyard offices. They managed payrolls, coordinated materials, and kept the vast enterprise running smoothly. In hindsight, the *Phoenix* was not just a product of American industry—it was a community effort, forged by the lives and labours of countless ordinary citizens.

## Launch and Commissioning

On 13 March 1938, USS *Phoenix* slid down the ways and touched the water for the first time. Her launch was marked by a traditional ceremony attended by naval dignitaries, political figures, and shipyard workers with their families. Champagne broke across her bow, and she entered the Delaware River to the roar of cheers and the blare of horns. To those present, it was a moment of pride and optimism, a tangible sign that the United States could build warships equal to any in the world.

When commissioned into service later that year, *Phoenix* officially joined the U.S. Navy's growing fleet. Her crew reported aboard, turning the silent steel into a living, breathing organism. Sailors quickly learned to navigate her labyrinth of compartments, from the mess decks and sleeping quarters deep within her hull to the gunnery stations and bridge high above the waterline. Life aboard a cruiser was cramped and often uncomfortable, but for many sailors, the *Phoenix* became home, a place where camaraderie and discipline defined daily existence.

## A Symbol of Preparedness

The commissioning of *Phoenix* came at a time when America's naval posture was still defensive and cautious. Congress debated budgets, isolationists decried entanglements abroad, and President Franklin D. Roosevelt sought a balance between domestic recovery and international readiness. Ships like *Phoenix* represented more than raw military power; they were political statements. Their presence reassured allies, deterred adversaries, and reminded Americans themselves that the nation was not defenceless should the world once again slide into war.

Across the Atlantic, Hitler's Germany continued to test the patience of Europe. In Asia, Japan's navy drilled relentlessly for the conflicts it anticipated. The *Phoenix* was thus launched into an environment of gathering storms. Her very existence spoke to the foresight of planners who recognised that war was not a distant possibility but a looming reality.

## Living Up to Her Name

The choice of name—*Phoenix*—would prove hauntingly appropriate. In mythology, the phoenix was a bird that burst into flames and was reborn from its own ashes, a symbol of resilience, renewal, and immortality. Though no one in 1938 could know the ship's eventual turbines. She was at peace, just another ship in a fleet confident in its might.

**The First Signs**

Just before 8 a.m., the illusion shattered. Aircraft engines—dozens of them—began to hum overhead, their sound unusual enough to draw sailors onto the decks. At first, some thought it was an American exercise; flights of planes often roared over Oahu. But when bombs began to fall and the rising sun insignia of Japan appeared on wings, disbelief turned to horror. The Japanese Imperial Navy had launched a surprise attack.

From *Phoenix's* vantage point, the scale of the assault was immediately clear. Torpedo planes skimmed low over the harbour, their deadly payloads streaking toward the great battleships moored along Battleship Row. Dive bombers screamed down from the clouds, releasing ordnance with terrifying accuracy. Within minutes, the proud USS *Arizona* erupted in a catastrophic explosion, her forward magazines igniting in a blast that shook the harbour. The *Oklahoma* rolled onto her side, capsizing with hundreds of sailors trapped inside. Oil fires spread across the water's surface, black smoke rising in choking plumes that blotted out the sun.

## Phoenix Under Attack

On board *Phoenix*, Captain Herman O. Stickney and his officers reacted swiftly. General quarters were sounded, klaxons blaring through the ship. Men sprinted to their battle stations, adrenaline surging as training took over. Gun crews scrambled to load the five-inch anti-aircraft guns, while others operated the 1.1-inch mounts and .50-calibre machine guns. Ammunition handlers formed human chains, hauling shells from magazines deep within the ship up to the waiting gunners above.

Within minutes, *Phoenix's* guns thundered into life. Her crew fired furiously at the swarms of Japanese planes diving and strafing overhead. Shells burst in black puffs of smoke, tracer rounds arced skyward, and the air filled with the deafening roar of battle. Sailors could see the gleaming undersides of enemy aircraft as they swooped low; some swore they could see the faces of the pilots. The ship shook under the recoil of her own guns, but she remained intact.

Unlike the lumbering battleships that made such tempting targets, the *Phoenix* was more difficult to hit. Her position in the harbour was less exposed, and the Japanese concentrated their efforts on the battleships and airfields that formed the backbone of American power in the Pacific. Even so, bomb fragments and strafing runs peppered her decks, and several sailors were injured. For hours, the crew fought on, their ship wrapped in smoke and the acrid stench of burning oil carried by the wind.

## A Lucky Ship

When the attack finally ended, Pearl Harbour was a scene of devastation. Over 2,400 Americans were dead, including 1,177 entombed in the shattered hull of the *Arizona*. Battleships lay sunk or burning, airfields were littered with wrecked planes, and the Pacific Fleet had been dealt a staggering blow. Yet *Phoenix* floated, scarred but unbroken. She had escaped severe damage, one of the few larger ships to emerge from the inferno largely intact.

To her crew, survival felt miraculous. They had stared death in the face, watched comrades perish on neighbouring ships, and endured an onslaught that could easily have claimed their own vessel. Sailors began to speak of their boat as "lucky," a reputation that would follow her through the war. But luck alone did not explain her survival. The crew's discipline, their swift response, and the cruiser's smaller profile all played a part. Together, these factors allowed *Phoenix* to steam defiantly out to sea that same afternoon, one of the first ships to do so.

## Into the Pacific

In the chaotic days that followed, the U.S. Navy scrambled to regroup. Rumours of Japanese invasion swirled around Hawaii, and every ship that could sail was pressed into service. The *Phoenix*, with her guns intact and her engines operational, became a vital asset. She patrolled the approaches to Oahu, scanning the seas for enemy carriers that might launch a second strike. Sailors, still shaken by what they had endured, worked with grim determination, knowing that the war they had hoped to avoid had come crashing down upon them.

In the weeks and months that followed, *Phoenix* settled into the unglamorous but essential duties of wartime service. She escorted convoys carrying troops and supplies across the Pacific, guarded aircraft carriers against submarine threats, and patrolled waters where Japanese raiders might lurk. For her crew, the learning curve was steep. Young sailors, many fresh from training schools, found themselves thrust into a global war. They learned the harsh routines of wartime sailing—endless drills, sleepless nights, and the constant vigilance required to survive in waters now prowled by enemy submarines and aircraft.

## A Reputation Forged

Though she did not immediately see the kind of headline-grabbing battles that defined the early months of the Pacific War, *Phoenix's* role was no less critical. Each convoy she escorted arrived safely, and each patrol she completed helped secure the fragile supply lines upon which victory depended. Slowly, the ship and her crew forged their reputation. She was not just a survivor of Pearl Harbour but an active participant in the fightback.

Her sailors took pride in being part of a ship with history already etched into her name. Letters home often mentioned the sense of destiny that clung to the *Phoenix*. "We were there when it started," one sailor wrote to his family. "Our ship came through when so many others didn't. I think we're meant to be part of whatever comes next." That feeling of destiny, of resilience, infused the crew with a sense of identity that carried them through the dark early years of the war.

## The Broader Symbolism

For the United States, the survival of ships like *Phoenix* carried symbolic weight. Amid the devastation of Pearl Harbour, stories of endurance were desperately needed. Newspaper reports highlighted the fact that not every boat had been destroyed, that the Pacific Fleet still had fight left in it. Photographs of cruisers and destroyers putting to sea gave the American public hope that all was not lost. *Phoenix* thus became more than just a ship—she was a reminder that resilience was possible, that America could and would rise from the ashes, much like her namesake bird.

## The Path Ahead

The attack on Pearl Harbour was the *Phoenix's* baptism by fire, an ordeal that seared itself into the memory of every sailor on board. It transformed the ship from a peacetime cruiser into a battle-hardened vessel, forged in the crucible of surprise and survival. From that day forward, her story would be one of relentless service across the Pacific, from the steaming jungles of New Guinea to the embattled islands of the Philippines.

Her crew would never forget 7 December. Each anniversary would be marked with solemn remembrance, the faces of fallen comrades haunting their memories. But they also carried with them a fierce pride: theirs was the ship that had faced the fury of Pearl Harbour and lived.

The USS *Phoenix* sailed into the wider war not as a symbol of defeat but as a harbinger of resilience. The flames that engulfed Pearl Harbour had baptised her, and from those flames she emerged ready to fight.

## Chapter 3: Pacific Warrior – Campaigns Against Japan

The USS *Phoenix* entered the war with the stigma and the honour of being a Pearl Harbour survivor. Her crew carried that memory forward like a badge, proud that their ship had endured while so many others lay in ruins. But survival was only the beginning. In the years that followed, *Phoenix* would become one of the Pacific Fleet's tireless workhorses, a ship rarely in the spotlight but always present in the long, grinding push from the South Pacific's jungles to the shores of the Philippines. She became known not for a single spectacular moment but for her consistency—the cruiser that could be relied upon to do the job, day after exhausting day, campaign after campaign.

## Into the War Zone

After the immediate aftermath of Pearl Harbour, *Phoenix* spent much of 1942 on escort and patrol duty, assignments that were crucial but rarely celebrated. Convoys carried troops, fuel, and supplies to the front lines, and Japanese submarines prowled the shipping lanes relentlessly. Protecting those lifelines was thankless work. Sailors learned to scan the waves for periscopes, to sleep lightly in case the klaxon sounded, and to live with the constant tension that at any moment a torpedo could rip through their hull. Yet *Phoenix* proved adept at the task, her sonar operators gaining sharp instincts and her gunners learning to respond in seconds to sudden threats from the sky.

The turning point came as the Allies shifted from defence to offence. By late 1942 and early 1943, the long island-hopping campaign began in earnest. General Douglas MacArthur in the Southwest Pacific and Admiral Chester Nimitz in the Central Pacific devised strategies to claw back territory from Japan, leapfrogging across chains of islands, isolating enemy garrisons, and establishing forward bases for the next push. Cruisers like *Phoenix* were indispensable to this strategy. They had the firepower to smash entrenched positions, the speed to keep up with carriers, and the endurance to operate for weeks in remote waters.

## New Guinea – Jungle Shorelines and Relentless Bombardments

One of *Phoenix's* earliest and most gruelling assignments was the New Guinea campaign. This vast, rugged island had been partially occupied by Japanese forces, who threatened Australia's northern approaches and sought to sever the lines of communication between America and its allies. In 1943, Allied operations turned toward driving them back.

*Phoenix*'s role was to provide naval gunfire support for amphibious landings. For sailors trained on gunnery ranges, the first time their six-inch shells screamed into dense jungle was a sobering moment. The Japanese were masters of concealment, digging bunkers deep into hillsides, camouflaging gun pits, and turning every ridge into a fortress. To break them, bombardments had to be relentless.

Hour after hour, *Phoenix's* guns roared, sending shells inland in carefully plotted patterns. The concussion rattled the ship's hull, and sailors stuffed cotton into their ears to dull the thunder. Spotter planes circled overhead, radioing back corrections to ensure the shells landed on target. The jungle trembled with the impacts, trees splintering, and earth erupting into geysers of mud and smoke. Yet often, when the smoke cleared, Japanese positions still fired back. It was a war of attrition, the ship's firepower smashing paths for infantry but never eliminating danger.

Life during these operations was a blur of action and exhaustion. Gunners sweated in the heat, their bodies streaked with grime, while cooks rushed meals to keep them fuelled. Below decks, the engine crews worked tirelessly to keep turbines humming, the heat and noise almost unbearable. When bombardments ended, sailors collapsed into hammocks, knowing that before long the call to battle stations would sound again.

**Shield and Spear**

In addition to bombardment, *Phoenix* often acted as both shield and spear in combined operations. As a shield, she screened vulnerable transports laden with troops and supplies. Japanese aircraft, flying from bases across the Pacific, frequently sought to disrupt landings with bombing runs or torpedo attacks. The cruiser's anti-aircraft gunners, already seasoned since Pearl Harbour, grew sharper with each encounter. Alarms would sound, and the decks erupted into controlled chaos—lookouts shouting bearings, directors calculating firing solutions, and gunners loosing streams of tracer fire skyward. Smoke and flame often marked the end of an enemy dive bomber, though the threat never ceased.

As a spear, *Phoenix* could unleash devastating salvos on coastal defences. During landings in places like Biak and Hollandia, she sailed close to shore, pounding beaches until they seemed to vanish in rolling waves of smoke. Troops later remembered the confidence they felt knowing cruisers like *Phoenix* had softened their targets. To the infantry slogging through mud and jungle, the sound of her shells overhead was a strange comfort, proof that they were not alone.

## Camaraderie in the Crucible

The ship became more than a war machine—it became a home. Long deployments at sea forged bonds that transcended rank or background. Sailors from farms in the Midwest, cities in the Northeast, and towns scattered across America found themselves living side by side in cramped quarters. They shared meals, jokes, and fears. They celebrated small victories, like receiving mail from home or managing a rare few hours of quiet at anchor. They mourned together when shipmates were lost in battle or accidents.

Stories circulated that *Phoenix* was charmed, her "luck" from Pearl Harbour following her into every fight. While other ships in the fleet sometimes fell victim to torpedoes or bombs, she seemed to come through unscathed. Superstition is a powerful thing at sea, and many sailors clung to the belief that their ship had destiny on her side. It bolstered morale when odds seemed overwhelming.

## Toward the Philippines

By 1944, the Allied advance pressed northward. New Guinea was secured mainly, and attention turned to the liberation of the Philippines. For *Phoenix*, this was both a strategic and symbolic campaign. The Philippines had fallen early in the war, and retaking them was essential to cutting Japan off from its southern resources.

MacArthur's famous promise to return would be fulfilled only through a massive naval and amphibious effort, and *Phoenix* was there in the thick of it.

During the Leyte Gulf operations in October 1944—the largest naval battle in history—*Phoenix* again played a key supporting role. She joined bombardment groups softening beaches for landings, her guns pounding Japanese defences. She also helped shield the invasion fleet from air attack. The skies above Leyte swarmed with Japanese aircraft, including the first organised kamikaze strikes. Sailors watched in horror as planes dove deliberately into American ships, exploding in fiery chaos. On *Phoenix*, gunners redoubled their efforts, cutting down attackers before they could strike. Each engagement left nerves frayed, but the ship held firm, her reputation as a reliable defender intact.

## Hard Service

The strain of continuous operations wore heavily on both ship and crew. The heat of constant gunfire scarred decks, paint blistered from the tropical sun, and machinery groaned under the relentless demands of war. Sailors endured extremes of exhaustion—long hours at battle stations, interrupted sleep, and monotonous meals hastily eaten between alarms. Disease, heat rash, and infections were constant threats in the humid climate. Yet the men endured, motivated by duty, camaraderie, and the knowledge that their efforts were pushing Japan back step by bloody step.

In letters home, they rarely spoke of fear. Instead, they mentioned the pride of being part of something larger, of contributing to a cause that spanned oceans. "We're tired, sure," one sailor wrote, "but when I see those troops go ashore under our guns, I know we're making a difference. That's enough to keep us going."

## Closing in on Japan

By 1945, *Phoenix* had helped pave the way through the Philippines and beyond. Though she was not present at every climactic moment of the Pacific War, her record of service was long and unbroken. She had fought in dozens of operations, each one part of the larger mosaic of the Allied advance. She was there when Japanese resistance stiffened, when kamikazes grew more desperate, and when the sea lanes gradually opened for the final assault on Japan's home islands.

Her contribution may not have made headlines in the newspapers back home—her name never had the fame of the *Enterprise* or the *Missouri*—but among the men who served on her and the commanders who relied upon her, *Phoenix* was a byword for reliability. She was the ship that turned up, did her job, and kept fighting.

## Reputation Secure

When the war finally drew to a close in August 1945, the crew of *Phoenix* could look back on nearly four years of continuous action. From the inferno of Pearl Harbour to the beaches of Leyte, she had sailed thousands of miles, fired countless rounds, and carried her men through the crucible of the Pacific. Her decks bore the scars of battle, her paint was faded, but her reputation was secure. She was no longer simply the "lucky ship" that had escaped destruction in Hawaii. She was a veteran in her own right, a gallant warrior of the Pacific.

## Chapter 4: Witness to Victory – The War's End

The summer of 1945 brought with it a sense of inevitability, though no one aboard USS *Phoenix* could afford complacency. After years of bitter campaigning across the Pacific—through New Guinea, the Philippines, and the endless chain of islands that marked Japan's outer defences—the end seemed near. Yet sailors knew that until surrender was signed, the danger was real. The Japanese military, battered but not broken, still possessed formidable forces, and rumours swirled of kamikaze attacks, last-ditch submarine raids, and the possibility of a climactic invasion of the home islands.

For the men of *Phoenix*, veterans now hardened by years of service, every day in 1945 carried a dual weight: the sense that they had come astonishingly far from the smoking ruins of Pearl Harbour, and the nagging fear that fate might yet claim them before peace was declared.

### Approaching the Endgame

By early 1945, *Phoenix* was operating with the Allied armadas that swept closer and closer to Japan itself. She took part in the operations that secured the Philippines, pounded Japanese coastal defences, and guarded convoys ferrying vital supplies. The Philippines campaign in particular had tested her crew's endurance. At Leyte Gulf, Samar, and Lingayen Gulf, her guns spoke in defence of landing forces, while her anti-aircraft crews fought wave after wave of kamikazes.

By the spring, the Allies had turned their attention to Okinawa. This island, lying scarcely 350 miles from the Japanese mainland, was considered a stepping stone to a possible invasion of Honshu. Though *Phoenix* herself did not bear the brunt of every engagement there, her role on the broader fleet was essential—escorting transports, bombarding positions, and contributing to the overwhelming firepower that slowly broke Japan's defensive ring.

It was in this context of relentless, bloody pressure that the atomic age dawned. News filtered through the fleet in August 1945: a single bomb had destroyed Hiroshima. A second bomb, dropped days later, devastated Nagasaki. Sailors aboard *Phoenix* struggled to comprehend the reports. Some were jubilant, convinced the weapon meant an immediate end to the war. Others were unsettled by the sheer scale of destruction described in sketchy communiqués. Whatever their private feelings, all knew the course of history had shifted.

## The Announcement of Surrender

On 15 August 1945, word reached the fleet that Emperor Hirohito had announced Japan's acceptance of surrender. For many on board *Phoenix*, the moment seemed almost unreal. Men gathered around radios, straining to catch the words. Some wept openly; others cheered, shouting themselves hoarse. For years, the thought of survival had been a daily struggle, not an assumption. Suddenly, the end was real. They had lived through the deadliest conflict in human history, and they had won.

Yet the war was not over in an instant. Sailors were reminded that Japan still possessed ships, submarines, and aircraft that might not immediately lay down arms. Orders went out to remain vigilant. Anti-aircraft watches stayed manned, and depth charges were kept ready. A single desperate act could still cost lives, and no commander wanted his ship to become the war's final casualty.

## Into Tokyo Bay

In late August and early September, *Phoenix* joined the great Allied armada that steamed into Tokyo Bay. The sight was extraordinary: a forest of masts, funnels, and flags from across the victorious nations, gathered in the heart of what had been enemy waters only weeks before. The towering presence of battleships such as USS *Missouri* dominated the skyline. Still, cruisers like *Phoenix* were no less important, their presence a reminder of the breadth of America's naval strength.

For her crew, entering Tokyo Bay was a moment of vindication. They remembered vividly the chaos of Pearl Harbour, the burning oil, the capsized hulls, and the disbelief that America's proud fleet had been humbled in a single morning. Now, four years later, they sailed into the enemy's capital, undefeated and unbowed. The symbolism was inescapable.

Sailors lined the rails, craning their necks to see the distant Japanese shoreline. Some whispered disbelief that they were truly here, alive, witnessing history. Others thought of shipmates lost along the way—men killed in New Guinea, at Leyte, or during endless patrols. Victory was sweet, but it carried the weight of sacrifice.

On 2 September 1945, the formal surrender ceremony took place on the deck of USS *Missouri*. Though *Phoenix* was not the stage for that event, her proximity made her a witness. The crew knew they were part of something larger than themselves—a fleet whose collective presence spoke louder than any individual ship. Together, they embodied the journey from defeat to triumph.

## The Symbolism of Survival

Of all the ships present in Tokyo Bay, *Phoenix* carried a unique symbolic resonance. She had been at Pearl Harbour on the day the war began for the United States, and now she was here at its end. From the first shock of torpedoes striking American battleships to the last salvos of bombardment along the Philippine coast, she had endured. Few ships could claim such a span of experience.

Her survival seemed almost uncanny to some. Sailors spoke of her as a "lucky ship," a vessel that had walked through fire and emerged unscathed. In truth, her endurance was a mixture of fortune, skill, and sheer determination. Crews had maintained her systems meticulously, commanders had employed her wisely, and her gunners had defended her fiercely. But myth and superstition cling to ships at sea, and for many, *Phoenix* had become a living talisman of resilience.

## Celebrations and Reflections

In the weeks following the surrender, *Phoenix* took part in occupation duties, patrolling Japanese waters, overseeing the disarmament of enemy vessels, and assisting in humanitarian missions. Yet the dominant mood aboard was one of release. Celebrations broke out, sometimes sanctioned, sometimes spontaneous. Bands struck up music on the deck, and sailors staged impromptu parties with whatever supplies could be spared.

Letters home carried the news: it was over, they were safe, and soon they would return. For families who had lived in uncertainty for years, these words were precious. Yet beneath the joy was a current of reflection. Many aboard were haunted by memories of lost friends and the sheer scale of destruction they had witnessed. Sailors who had stood watch as kamikazes plunged into nearby ships or who had seen cities reduced to rubble carried those images with them long after the cheering faded.

## A Navy in Transition

Victory also meant change. The massive wartime fleet that had carried America to triumph could not be sustained in peacetime. The dozen decommissioned ships are either mothballed in the reserve fleet or scrapped. Crews were demobilised, returning to civilian life in a nation eager to turn from war to peace.

For *Phoenix*, the writing was on the wall. Though still a modern ship by some standards, she was part of a class already considered less advanced than the newer cruisers and carriers that dominated naval strategy. The US Navy, looking ahead to the challenges of the Cold

War, prioritised aircraft carriers, submarines, and radar-equipped vessels over traditional gunnery cruisers.

By late 1946, orders were issued for her decommissioning. For many of her crew, this news was bittersweet. They had invested years of their lives in her steel hull, and she had carried them safely through countless dangers. To think of her lying up, silent and empty, seemed almost unnatural. Yet such was the cycle of naval service: ships, like men, had their time.

## Remembered as a Veteran

Before leaving service, *Phoenix* was recognised as a veteran of distinction. She received nine battle stars for her World War II service, a record that testified to her continuous and active participation in the Pacific campaign. Ceremonies marked her achievements, with dignitaries and naval officers praising her resilience and her crew's dedication.

For the men who had served aboard her, the honours were welcome but secondary. What mattered was that they had done their duty and survived. In reunions years later, veterans often spoke not of medals or stars but of the friendships forged, the nights endured, and the relief of seeing land again after endless weeks at sea. *Phoenix* had been their world, and she remained fixed in their memories as both a home and a crucible.

## The End of an American Chapter

By the time she was officially decommissioned, USS *Phoenix* had already secured her place in history. She had begun as a product of the interwar treaties and shipbuilding programmes, had survived the crucible of Pearl Harbour, and had carried her guns into nearly every major campaign of the Pacific War. She ended her American career as a witness to Japan's surrender, a symbol of resilience and victory.

Yet her story was not finished. While the US Navy prepared to place her in reserve, another nation looked upon her steel hull with interest. The postwar years would see her reborn, sold to Argentina, and given a new name and identity. But before that chapter began, she remained, for a brief moment, a proud American cruiser basking in the afterglow of victory.

For her crew, those final days in Tokyo Bay and beyond were indelible. They had entered the war as young men—some scarcely out of school—and emerged as veterans of one of the most brutal conflicts in history. They had sailed thousands of miles, fought in innumerable battles, and seen the world change before their eyes. Through it all, *Phoenix* had been their constant companion.

And so, as they looked back on their time aboard, they knew they had been part of something extraordinary. Their ship, like the mythical bird whose name she bore, had risen from the ashes of Pearl Harbour to soar across the Pacific, only to stand proudly in Tokyo Bay as the guns fell silent.

## Chapter 5: From Phoenix to Belgrano – Transfer to Argentina

The guns of the Second World War had fallen silent, but their echoes lingered in the fleets that filled naval bases from San Diego to Sydney. By the early 1950s, the United States possessed a navy larger than the rest of the world combined. Battleships, carriers, cruisers, and destroyers crowded harbours, many now redundant in the dawn of the atomic age. Aircraft carriers and submarines, with their ability to project nuclear and conventional power, were fast becoming the true symbols of maritime dominance. The once-proud cruisers that had fought at Guadalcanal, Leyte Gulf, and Okinawa seemed outdated, even though most were still sound hulls with decades of service left in them.

It was a time of downsizing, and America faced the question of what to do with these steel leviathans. Scrapping them was expensive and politically unappealing, while mothballing entire fleets consumed space and resources. The solution, in many cases, was transfer. Allies across the globe—some war-torn, others emerging powers—were eager to acquire ships that would bolster their fleets at a fraction of the cost of new construction. For Washington, selling or loaning vessels also offered diplomatic benefits, binding nations into closer security relationships during the nascent Cold War.

Among the ships marked for transfer was the *Phoenix*, a veteran of Pearl Harbour and Tokyo Bay. Decommissioned in 1946 and placed in reserve at Philadelphia, she lay in quiet limbo for five years, her decks empty, her boilers cold. Yet even in silence, she remained a valuable asset. And in Buenos Aires, across the equator, the Argentine Navy was watching.

## Argentina's Naval Ambitions

For Argentina, the early 1950s were a period of ambition and change. Under President Juan Domingo Perón, the nation sought to establish itself not merely as a regional player but as a modern state capable of commanding respect on the world stage. Perón's government invested heavily in industry, infrastructure, and military modernisation. Central to this vision was the navy.

Argentina had long viewed itself as a maritime nation, with thousands of miles of Atlantic coastline and a proud tradition of naval service stretching back to the wars of independence. But by the mid-twentieth century, its fleet was ageing. Ships built before or during the First World War still formed the backbone of its naval power, and compared to its neighbours—particularly Brazil, which was also modernising—Argentina risked slipping behind.

The acquisition of modern warships was therefore both practical and symbolic. To command the South Atlantic and safeguard Argentina's economic lifelines, the navy needed ships capable of standing alongside those of global powers. To the Perón government, buying an American cruiser was not just about firepower; it was about prestige, the ability to declare that Argentina's flag flew from the deck of a vessel that had witnessed history.

## The Sale and the Name

In 1951, negotiations concluded. USS *Phoenix* was sold to Argentina under a broader programme of American military assistance. She was formally transferred in October of that year, and with her new identity came a new name: *General Belgrano*.

The choice was deeply symbolic. Manuel Belgrano was one of Argentina's founding fathers, a general, economist, and politician who had fought for independence from Spain in the early nineteenth century. He was also credited with designing the Argentine flag, a symbol of unity and national pride. By naming the cruiser after him, Argentina tied the ship directly to its national identity, binding her steel hull to the story of independence and sovereignty. She was no longer simply a foreign vessel purchased second-hand; she was reborn as an Argentine icon.

To the sailors who would crew her, the renaming ceremony carried profound meaning. Many of them were young men who had never set foot outside South America, and now they were preparing to take charge of a ship that had steamed across the Pacific, survived Pearl Harbour, and witnessed Japan's surrender. Standing at attention as the Stars and Stripes were lowered and the sky-blue and white flag of Argentina was raised, they felt the weight of history shift. The ship was theirs now—her decks, her turrets, her engines. She would sail under their command, embodying their nation's pride.

## Arrival in Argentina

The voyage south from American waters to Buenos Aires was both a shakedown cruise and a symbolic journey. As the cruiser approached Argentine shores, crowds gathered at the docks to witness her arrival. Newspapers heralded her as proof of Argentina's growing naval strength, running photographs of her bristling guns and sleek silhouette.

When *General Belgrano* sailed up the River Plate, past the skyline of Buenos Aires, she was greeted with pageantry. Bands played, dignitaries saluted, and sailors' families craned their necks to catch a glimpse of the ship that was suddenly the pride of the fleet. For the Argentine Navy, this was a watershed moment: they had acquired not just any vessel, but a veteran of the greatest war in human history. The symbolic power of this was immense.

On board, Argentine officers walked the same decks that American sailors had trodden in battle. They touched the breech of the six-inch guns that had fired at Japanese positions, examined the scars left by shrapnel and time, and began to write their own chapter in her history.

## Training a New Crew

Integrating the *Belgrano* into the Argentine Navy was no simple task. American ships were designed with American systems, manuals, and procedures, and Argentine sailors needed months of training to familiarise themselves with their operations. Technical manuals had to be translated, and equipment adapted to local practices. US Navy advisors assisted, but much of the work was left to the Argentine crew themselves.

Young sailors, many scarcely out of the naval academy, learned to operate the great turrets, to manage the engine rooms, and to navigate the cruiser's complex electrical systems. For them, serving aboard *Belgrano* was both a challenge and an honour. She was larger and more potent than anything many of them had ever seen, a ship that demanded discipline and teamwork.

Veterans of Argentina's older ships marvelled at her capabilities. Her radar systems, though already beginning to age by American standards, were advanced compared to those in the Argentine fleet. Her speed and firepower gave the navy a deterrent value it had lacked. She was, in every sense, a leap forward.

## A Symbol of National Pride

Throughout the 1950s and 1960s, *General Belgrano* became a fixture of Argentina's naval presence. She sailed in fleet exercises, patrolled the South Atlantic, and represented Argentina in international visits. Photographs of her appeared in school textbooks and newspapers, and she was often featured in naval parades and commemorations.

For Argentina's people, she became a source of pride. Veterans of the War of Independence had marched beneath banners of Belgrano the man; now their descendants watched a steel giant sail under his name. She embodied not just naval strength but national sovereignty, a reminder that Argentina was no minor player in the South Atlantic.

## A Vessel Between Eras

Yet even as she served proudly, the *Belgrano* was already a ship caught between eras. Built in the 1930s, she had been designed for a kind of naval warfare that was rapidly becoming obsolete. Her guns, formidable though they were, could not match the reach or versatility of carrier aircraft or guided missiles. Naval doctrine in the Cold War shifted toward submarines, carriers, and missile cruisers. The *Belgrano* was a gun cruiser in a missile age.

Still, she had her uses. Her very size and presence carried deterrent power, and for the Argentine Navy, she was invaluable as a training ship and a symbol. In peacetime manoeuvres, her silhouette on the horizon told friend and foe alike that Argentina could still field a vessel of significant firepower.

## Politics and the Navy

Her arrival was also intertwined with Argentina's turbulent politics. The Perón years were marked by both populist pride and deep divisions. The navy, often at odds with Perón, nonetheless benefited from his modernisation efforts. After Perón's ousting in 1955, the navy played a significant role in political life, and the *Belgrano* remained part of its arsenal.

At times, she carried presidents and dignitaries, a floating embassy of Argentine power. At other times, she was a training ground, preparing sailors for the possibility of war. Through coups, protests, and economic turmoil, she remained a constant presence—grey, silent, yet symbolic.

**Echoes of the Past**

For those who remembered her American days, the transformation was poignant. Former US Navy sailors occasionally corresponded with their Argentine counterparts, sharing memories of wartime service. Some travelled to Buenos Aires years later to see the ship they had once called home, marvelling at her new flag and her new role.

In Argentina, she gained new layers of identity. To older veterans, she was a symbol of international recognition, proof that Argentina had risen to possess a ship with such a distinguished pedigree. To younger sailors, she was simply *Belgrano*, their boat, as familiar as the streets of Buenos Aires.

**Setting the Stage for Tragedy**

By the late 1970s and early 1980s, the *Belgrano* was showing her age. Her systems required constant maintenance, and by global standards, she was outdated. Yet she remained in commission, still sailing the South Atlantic, still representing Argentine pride. Few could have imagined that this second life, begun with such optimism, would end in such sudden tragedy in 1982.

## Chapter 6: A Latin American Power – Service in Argentina

When the *General Belgrano* entered Argentine service in 1951, she was more than a new addition to the navy's order of battle. She was a statement: a declaration that Argentina was determined to stand tall in the South Atlantic and project power across Latin America. For the next three decades, she would embody that ambition. She did not fight great battles like she had under the Stars and Stripes, but her very presence as a war veteran of Pearl Harbour and the Pacific carried weight. In Argentina's navy, she was not simply a ship—she was a floating banner of prestige.

### Training a New Generation

In the 1950s and 60s, the Argentine Navy underwent a significant transformation. Many of its older ships, dating back to the First World War, were slowly retired, and vessels like the *Belgrano* became the backbone of training and readiness. Thousands of sailors passed through her decks during these decades, learning navigation, gunnery, engineering, and the traditions of life at sea.

Life aboard was rigorous. Recruits endured long hours of drills, maintenance, and watch duties. They learned to climb the ladders to the high turrets, to polish brass fittings until they gleamed, and to keep the massive six-inch guns in working order even though the likelihood of firing them in anger was remote. The ship's engineers spent days in the hot, deafening engine rooms, coaxing her boilers and turbines into steady performance. Every voyage was a lesson, every exercise a rehearsal for duties that might never come. Yet for sailors who donned the Argentine uniform, serving aboard the *Belgrano* was a mark of pride. She was their fleet's flagship in spirit if not always in fact.

## A Tool of Diplomacy

Beyond her training role, the *Belgrano* became a vital instrument of diplomacy. Argentina recognised that the projection of naval power was not always about combat—it was about presence. When the *Belgrano* entered a foreign port, she carried not only her sailors but also the prestige of the Argentine state.

Throughout the 1950s and 1960s, she undertook numerous cruises to Brazil, Uruguay, and Chile, as well as goodwill visits further afield. On these voyages, she hosted receptions for diplomats, foreign officers, and local dignitaries. Her decks were dressed with flags, her brasswork polished until it shone, and her crew stood in immaculate formation as visitors climbed the gangway. In such moments, she was less a warship than a floating embassy, demonstrating Argentina's commitment to regional cooperation—or, when necessary, its resolve to stand firm.

## A Symbol of Prestige

The psychological impact of the *Belgrano*'s presence cannot be overstated. In Buenos Aires, schoolchildren learned of her in their lessons, and newspapers frequently carried photographs of her entering or leaving port. For a public often distracted by the turbulence of national politics—Perón's downfall in 1955, the succession of military and civilian governments that followed—the navy's great cruiser offered continuity. She represented something enduring and influential, a source of national pride afloat.

At naval parades and commemorations, she was often the centrepiece. Her guns would thunder in salute, echoing across the River Plate, and spectators would marvel at the grey giant whose silhouette dominated the horizon. To many Argentines, she was proof that their nation belonged among the world's maritime powers.

## The Chilean Rivalry

The 1960s and 1970s brought simmering tensions with Chile, Argentina's long-standing rival over disputed borderlands in Patagonia and the Beagle Channel. While open war never broke out, naval shows of strength became an essential tool of deterrence. In this context, the *Belgrano* was a powerful symbol.

On manoeuvres in the southern Atlantic, her presence sent an unmistakable message. Even if she was no longer the cutting edge of naval warfare, her size and firepower made her a formidable adversary for any regional navy. Chile's navy, smaller and less well-equipped, could not ignore the psychological advantage Argentina held simply by maintaining a ship of her stature.

In several tense moments—particularly during the Beagle Channel dispute of the late 1970s—the Argentine Navy deployed its most visible assets as part of its posture. The *Belgrano*, along with aircraft carriers and destroyers, patrolled southern waters, making Argentina's naval strength visible in the contested seas. Though she never fired a shot in anger during these disputes, her role as a deterrent was fundamental. Diplomats and generals in Santiago took her into account when weighing their options.

## Modernisation and Limitations

By the 1960s, however, the *Belgrano* was beginning to show her age. Naval technology was evolving rapidly, and missile systems, radar, and nuclear submarines were rewriting the rules of sea power. The Argentine Navy did what it could to keep her relevant. Upgrades were made to her radar and communications, and her anti-aircraft defences were strengthened with more modern weapons. Engineers worked tirelessly to keep her engines reliable and her systems functional.

Yet there was no disguising the fact that she was a cruiser designed in the 1930s. Her six-inch guns were powerful, but in an era of jet aircraft and guided missiles, they were increasingly obsolete. Maintaining her required constant effort and resources. Still, Argentina kept her in service, not because she was the most modern warship in the fleet, but because she remained its most visible symbol.

## Sailors' Lives

For the sailors who served aboard her, the *Belgrano* was a home as much as a duty. Her mess decks echoed with laughter, arguments, and songs. Her wardroom saw young officers grow into seasoned leaders. She carried generations of sailors down the coast of South America, across the Atlantic, and into distant ports.

Stories circulated in naval circles of the *Belgrano*'s quirks—the stubborn machinery that required coaxing, the gun crews who competed to see who could strip and reassemble a breech fastest, the camaraderie of long nights on watch under southern skies. Many sailors spoke of her not in terms of obsolescence but affection. She was their ship, their pride, their proving ground.

## A Political Symbol

During Argentina's turbulent political history of the 1960s and 1970s, the *Belgrano* also played a quieter political role. Naval parades and displays of strength were often used by governments—civilian and military alike—to bolster legitimacy. When the *Belgrano* steamed past crowds in Buenos Aires, flags flying, she projected an image of national unity and power that contrasted with the instability ashore.

In times of economic hardship, she was a reminder of Argentina's enduring capability. In times of political crisis, she was a symbol of continuity. Whether consciously or not, governments used her as a stage prop for their own authority.

## Regional Balance

In Latin America's naval balance of power, the *Belgrano* carried real weight. Brazil's navy was larger overall, but Argentina's possession of a Brooklyn-class cruiser gave it a visible prestige asset. Other nations in the region, lacking comparable ships, could not match the visual or symbolic impact of the *Belgrano*'s presence.

Thus, throughout the Cold War decades, she played her part in maintaining Argentina's naval reputation. She was not a frontline asset against superpowers, but she did not need to be. Her function was regional, and in that role she succeeded admirably.

## Preparing for the Future

By the late 1970s, whispers of obsolescence grew louder. The Argentine Navy debated whether to retire her, to convert her into a training ship permanently, or to continue deploying her as a deterrent. Maintenance costs were rising, and the challenges of integrating her into a missile-dominated world were mounting. Yet her symbolic value argued for her retention.

She remained in service, her hull carrying both history and aspiration. When she steamed into the southern Atlantic on exercises, she was both a relic of the past and a reminder of Argentina's determination to remain a naval power. No sailor, no admiral, and certainly no politician could look at her without sensing the weight of her story.

## Chapter 7: Cold War Currents – A Navy in Transition

The decades after the Second World War were shaped by Cold War rivalries, shifting alliances, and the technological revolution in military affairs. For the Argentine Navy, and for its venerable cruiser *General Belgrano*, this was both an era of opportunity and challenge. The ship that had once braved Pearl Harbour and fought through the Pacific was now repurposed as a tool of national pride and deterrence in South America. Yet as the Cold War deepened, her very presence in the fleet began to reveal the contradictions of Argentina's naval ambitions: she was at once a powerful symbol and a stubborn anachronism.

### A Ship of Two Worlds

By the late 1950s and early 1960s, *Belgrano* was already something of a paradox. In South America, she was an impressive asset. Few of Argentina's regional neighbours could boast of such a large and heavily armed cruiser. Her fifteen-six-inch guns, spread across five turrets, gave her formidable firepower against surface targets. Her size, endurance, and prestige placed her at the heart of the Argentine fleet, often serving as a command ship during exercises and patrols.

But on the world stage, things looked different. The naval revolution unleashed by the Second World War was still unfolding. Aircraft carriers, jet aircraft, submarines, and guided missiles were rewriting the rules of sea power. In such a world, a gun cruiser designed in the 1930s was increasingly out of step. Where once she had been a symbol of modernity, by the Cold War era, she was showing her age.

## The Technological Gap

The arrival of guided missiles highlighted *Belgrano*'s limitations. By the 1960s, both NATO and Warsaw Pact navies were equipping their fleets with anti-ship missiles, surface-to-air systems, and long-range radars. A single rocket, launched from beyond the horizon, could disable or destroy a ship like *Belgrano* in moments—something her armour and gun batteries were never designed to counter.

Argentina attempted to modernise where possible. New radar systems were installed, communications equipment upgraded, and her anti-aircraft batteries reinforced. She remained seaworthy, her engines kept alive through constant maintenance, and her gunnery still sharp during exercises. Yet the core of her design could not be altered. She remained a cruiser from the 1930s, ill-suited to fight in a missile-dominated environment.

This reality did not go unnoticed by naval officers. Many younger commanders, trained in NATO academies or alongside allied fleets, recognised that Argentina's long-term security required investment in modern systems—missile-armed destroyers, submarines, and aircraft. Still, senior officers and politicians clung to *Belgrano*. Her prestige, her presence, and her history made her too valuable as a symbol to let go.

## The Politics of Prestige

Argentina's turbulent politics played a significant role in keeping *Belgrano* active. The nation oscillated between civilian governments and military juntas, and the armed forces became central to political life. For successive regimes, naval power was more than just defence—it was a projection of legitimacy, authority, and ambition.

Whenever *Belgrano* sailed into Buenos Aires, flags flying and guns saluting, she reminded the public of Argentina's maritime heritage and military strength. She was a tool of theatre as much as strategy, paraded before the nation on Navy Day, used as a backdrop for speeches, and featured in newsreels and newspapers. For a junta eager to display its strength, maintaining *Belgrano* was worth the cost. She embodied permanence and power in a nation often plagued by instability.

## Regional Rivalries

Regional tensions also justified her continued service. Argentina's long-standing rivalry with Chile over border disputes in Patagonia and, more critically, the Beagle Channel, reached dangerous levels in the

1970s. Naval shows of strength were routine. Warships from both sides patrolled contested waters, their presence a warning and a deterrent.

In this context, *Belgrano* still carried weight. She might not have been able to stand against a NATO fleet, but against Chilean destroyers and frigates, she remained formidable. Her size, her guns, and her symbolic power gave Argentina confidence. When deployed during tense standoffs, her silhouette alone sent a message. Chile could not ignore her presence, even if modern technology meant she was more vulnerable than her imposing appearance suggested.

## A Floating School and Ambassador

By the 1960s, the *Belgrano* had become more than a combat unit—she was also a training ground and a diplomatic platform. Thousands of Argentine sailors learned their craft aboard her decks. From navigation to gunnery, engineering to seamanship, she trained generations who would go on to crew newer ships and submarines.

She also undertook goodwill cruises, visiting Brazil, Uruguay, and occasionally further afield. These voyages showcased Argentina's naval presence, strengthening ties with allies and demonstrating that Buenos Aires remained committed to its role as a regional power. In such moments, she was more useful as a floating embassy than as a warship, hosting receptions, entertaining dignitaries, and flying the Argentine flag proudly abroad.

## The Costs of Nostalgia

Keeping her active, however, came at a price. Maintenance grew increasingly expensive. Spare parts were difficult to obtain, and crews often had to improvise solutions to keep her engines and systems functioning. Dockyard periods grew longer, and every voyage was preceded by weeks of repairs.

Critics within the navy argued that the resources spent on *Belgrano* could have been better invested in modern missile destroyers or submarines. Yet others pointed out that Argentina lacked the budget to replace her outright. Until a new fleet could be built or purchased, *Belgrano* remained a valuable deterrent in the South Atlantic. Her upkeep, they argued, was the price of maintaining prestige in a competitive regional environment.

## Cold War Alignments

The Cold War added another layer of complexity. Argentina was officially non-aligned, yet it leaned at times toward the United States and at others toward a more independent or even adversarial stance. For Washington, transferring older ships like the Phoenix to Latin American allies was part of a broader strategy of containing Soviet influence. For Argentina, accepting such ships was an opportunity to modernise cheaply while asserting independence.

The *Belgrano* thus became a Cold War asset in more ways than one. Though she never faced Soviet ships directly, her role in regional waters was part of the larger balance. She reminded neighbouring states that Argentina's navy, however outdated, could still project a significant force. She also symbolised Argentina's ability to act independently, maintaining its own sphere of influence in the South Atlantic and Antarctic approaches.

**The Human Side**

For her crew, the Cold War years were a mixture of pride and frustration. Sailors took pride in serving on one of the Navy's most historic and prestigious ships. Many spoke of the honour of walking her decks, knowing she had survived Pearl Harbour and carried a legacy few other ships could match.

But they also felt the frustrations of serving on an ageing vessel. Life aboard was cramped, noisy, and hot. Systems broke down with frustrating regularity, and sailors often spent more time repairing machinery than training for combat. The younger generation, aware of modern ships abroad, sometimes joked that they were serving on a "museum with guns." Yet despite the grumbles, loyalty to the *Belgrano* remained strong. She had a character of her own, and crews came to love her quirks as much as they cursed them.

## A Navy in Transition

By the late 1970s, Argentina's navy was caught between two eras. On the one hand, it was acquiring modern vessels—missile-armed destroyers, submarines, and even an aircraft carrier. On the other hand, it still relied heavily on older warships like the *Belgrano*. This dual identity reflected both ambition and reality: Argentina wanted to be seen as a modern maritime power, but it could not yet afford to discard the past.

The *Belgrano* thus became the embodiment of this transition. She was a bridge between eras, a ship that carried the traditions of battleships and cruisers into a world of missiles and jets. She was admired, but also questioned. Her very presence in the fleet symbolised both Argentina's naval pride and its limitations.

## A Symbol Too Valuable to Lose

Ultimately, the reason she endured into the 1980s was not strictly strategic—it was symbolic. Nations do not part easily with icons, and the *Belgrano* was an icon of Argentina's navy. Retiring her would have meant conceding that the country's ambitions outstripped its means.

Keeping her afloat allowed Argentina to continue projecting an image of power and continuity.

And so she remained in service, even as the world around her changed. She drilled, trained, patrolled, and hosted dignitaries. She steamed south into disputed waters and returned to Buenos Aires in triumph. She remained a paradox—still formidable in appearance, yet increasingly vulnerable in reality.

## Chapter 8: The Falklands Prelude – Sailing into Tension

In the spring of 1982, the cruiser that had once been launched as USS *Phoenix* and reborn as ARA *General Belgrano* sailed into the South Atlantic for what would be the last mission of her storied career. More than four decades after her keel had first been laid, she was once again at the centre of world attention. For Argentina, she represented a proud link to past glories and a symbol of national strength. For Britain, she was a looming threat, a powerful reminder that Argentina still possessed the ability to contest the seas. For the men who served aboard her, she was home—an ageing but trusted warship, her steel decks echoing with history. As tensions over the Falkland Islands flared into open conflict, *Belgrano* was propelled into the heart of the crisis, embodying both the ambition and the vulnerability of Argentina's junta.

### The Road to War

The Falkland Islands, or *Islas Malvinas* as Argentina calls them, had long been a point of contention. Britain had administered them since the nineteenth century, but Argentina never relinquished its claim. In the late 1970s and early 1980s, as Argentina struggled under economic decline and political unrest, the ruling military junta saw the islands as an opportunity. Reclaiming the Malvinas promised to ignite patriotic fervour and distract from domestic failures.

On 2 April 1982, Argentine troops landed on the islands, overwhelming the small British garrison. For the junta, led by General Leopoldo Galtieri, it was a bold move. Crowds filled the streets of Buenos Aires, waving flags and cheering the "recovery" of the Malvinas. Yet the triumph was short-lived. In London, Prime Minister Margaret Thatcher's government resolved to retake the islands. A British task force was rapidly assembled, its carriers, destroyers, and nuclear submarines steaming south into the Atlantic.

As the two nations prepared for conflict, the Argentine Navy found itself at the centre of strategy. Its ships would be vital in deterring or, if necessary, attacking the British fleet. Among them was the *Belgrano*, her name still resonant with pride, but her reality that of an ageing warship from another era.

## A Symbol of Naval Power

For Argentina's leaders, deploying *Belgrano* was both practical and symbolic. On paper, she remained a powerful vessel. Her fifteen six-inch guns could deliver devastating fire against surface targets or bombard coastal positions. She was heavily armoured compared to modern frigates, and her size made her an imposing presence on the open sea.

Yet her real power was symbolic. She was the Navy's elder statesman, a ship steeped in history. Many Argentines knew of her survival at Pearl Harbour, her long service under the U.S. flag, and her transformation into a national asset. In speeches and newspapers, her deployment was framed as a patriotic gesture—proof that Argentina would defend its claims with courage and resolve.

For the sailors who crewed her, that symbolism carried weight. The average age aboard was startlingly young; many conscripts were teenagers, barely trained and far from home. They looked up to the seasoned officers and petty officers who had guided the ship through decades of service. To the young men, the *Belgrano* was more than steel—it was a rite of passage, a trial by fire they had not expected to face but which they accepted with a mixture of fear and pride.

## The Challenges of an Ageing Cruiser

Behind the symbolism, however, lay cold realities. By 1982, *Belgrano* was outdated. Her systems, though maintained with dedication, belonged to another generation. She lacked modern radar and electronic countermeasures capable of detecting or defeating the latest missile threats. She carried no anti-ship missiles of her own, relying entirely on her gun batteries. And while she had some anti-aircraft capability, it was no match for supersonic jets armed with modern weapons.

The most pressing danger came from below the waves. Nuclear-powered submarines, like those Britain deployed to the South Atlantic, could operate silently for weeks, stalking targets across vast distances. For a ship like *Belgrano*, built in an era before such submarines existed, this was a peril for which no amount of gunnery practice could compensate. Her escorts—two destroyers armed with Exocet missiles—provided some protection, but the vulnerability remained.

Argentine admirals knew this. Some questioned whether it was wise to deploy her into contested waters. Yet the junta pressed ahead. To withhold her would look like weakness. To deploy her was to project confidence. And so, despite the risks, *Belgrano* sailed south.

**Into the South Atlantic**

In mid-April 1982, *Belgrano* joined Argentina's main naval forces. She became part of Task Group 79.3, patrolling the southern approaches to the Falklands. The British had declared a Total Exclusion Zone around the islands, warning that any Argentine ship or aircraft entering it could be attacked. *Belgrano* operated just outside that zone, shadowing the British fleet and waiting for orders.

The conditions at sea were harsh. The South Atlantic in autumn was a world away from the tropics of Pearl Harbour. Storms swept across the ocean, waves battered decks, and the cold penetrated steel bulkheads. For many of the young conscripts, it was their first experience of such unforgiving seas. Seasickness was common, but so too was a growing sense of anticipation. They knew they were at war, even if the first shots had yet to be fired.

## A Crew Divided by Experience

Life aboard reflected the ship's dual character: a seasoned veteran manned by youthful novices. The officers, many of whom had decades of naval service, carried themselves with calm authority. They drilled the crew, ran gunnery exercises, and prepared for the possibility of combat. To them, *Belgrano* was a trusted vessel, her quirks well known, her resilience proven.

The conscripts, however, lived in a world of rumour and uncertainty. Many came from inland towns and villages; the sea was alien to them. They whispered about the British fleet, about aircraft carriers and nuclear submarines. Some were proud to be part of history, while others confessed to fear in letters home. What united them was a sense of duty—whatever their personal feelings, they were part of the crew now, bound to the fate of the ship.

## The Gamble of Deployment

For Argentina's admirals, *Belgrano*'s deployment was a calculated risk. On one hand, she added weight to the fleet, her guns still capable of wreaking havoc on lighter British ships. On the other hand, she was a target—slow compared to submarines and vulnerable to modern weapons.

The junta, however, saw only the potential benefits. Her presence tied down British resources, forcing London to allocate submarines to shadow her and surface ships to guard against her. She was, in effect, a strategic distraction as much as a fighting unit. By keeping her at sea, Argentina hoped to stretch the British task force thin, complicating its already difficult mission.

## A Symbol of Pride and Peril

In Buenos Aires, state media reported proudly on the fleet's movements. Photographs of *Belgrano* appeared in newspapers, her profile unmistakable, her decks crowded with sailors waving at the cameras. She became a rallying symbol, proof that Argentina's navy was committed to the struggle.

Yet privately, some within the Navy worried. They knew that, in a clash with Britain's nuclear submarines or carrier-based aircraft, *Belgrano* could not hope to survive. They argued that her best use was symbolic, not operational. But the junta dismissed such caution. For leaders desperate to maintain the momentum of national enthusiasm, hesitation was unacceptable.

## Sailing Toward Destiny

And so, as April turned to May, *Belgrano* continued her patrols, her course taking her further into the cold South Atlantic. Her guns were operational, her crew was drilled, and her escorts were alert. She was both an active participant in the unfolding drama and a vessel caught by history, her fate tied to decisions made far beyond her steel decks.

To the young conscripts, she was invincible, a giant of the sea whose sheer size and history made her seem untouchable. To her officers, she was brave but vulnerable, a relic sailing in a modern war. To Argentina, she was pride incarnate. To Britain, she was a threat that could not be ignored.

The prelude was nearly over. The storm clouds of battle gathered on the horizon. And *General Belgrano*, once the lucky *Phoenix* of Pearl Harbour, now sailed once more into the unknown—into tension, into danger, and toward her final chapter.

## Chapter 9: Tragedy in the South Atlantic – The Sinking

On 2 May 1982, the long life of the warship that had begun as USS *Phoenix* came to its violent end. In the grey, freezing waters of the South Atlantic, the cruiser now known as ARA *General Belgrano* was struck by torpedoes from the British nuclear-powered submarine HMS *Conqueror*. Within twenty minutes, she rolled and sank, taking 323 Argentine sailors to their deaths. It was one of the most consequential and controversial naval actions of the late twentieth century—hailed in London as a decisive blow, mourned in Buenos Aires as a national tragedy, and debated internationally as a question of legality and morality.

## The Shadow Below

By late April, the British task force had reached the South Atlantic, prepared to contest Argentina's occupation of the Falklands. Prime Minister Margaret Thatcher and her war cabinet were acutely aware of the threat posed by the Argentine Navy. While British carriers and destroyers were formidable, they could not withstand a coordinated strike by Argentina's cruisers and missile-armed destroyers. A single success by the Argentines—say, the destruction of a British carrier—could have changed the balance of the war.

To mitigate that risk, Britain deployed nuclear-powered submarines to shadow Argentine warships. Among them was HMS *Conqueror*, a Churchill-class attack submarine. Powered by a nuclear reactor, she could remain submerged for months, moving silently beneath the waves at speeds unimaginable for conventional diesel-electric submarines. Her mission was to monitor and, if ordered, strike Argentina's surface fleet.

For days, *Conqueror* had stalked the *Belgrano* and her two escorts, the destroyers *Hippólito Bouchard* and *Piedra Buena*. The submariners aboard her listened to the rhythm of propellers through sonar, tracking the ships in the darkness of the deep. It was a contest of patience: a hunter waiting for permission to strike, a target unaware that death travelled with her just beneath the waves.

## The Decision in London

The decision to attack was not taken lightly. The British had declared a 200-nautical-mile Total Exclusion Zone around the Falklands, warning that any Argentine vessel entering it risked destruction. On 2 May, however, the *Belgrano* was just outside that zone, heading westward, as if returning toward the Argentine mainland.

In Whitehall, the dilemma was stark. Allowing her to continue might mean she would later turn back and threaten the task force. Sinking her, however, would raise questions: was it justified to attack a ship outside the exclusion zone, moving away from the islands?

Margaret Thatcher's war cabinet weighed the intelligence. British signals intercepts suggested the Argentine fleet was manoeuvring for a coordinated pincer attack on the task force, with *Belgrano* approaching from the south. At the same time, carrier-based aircraft struck from the north. Even as she steamed away, she remained within striking distance should orders change. The stakes were too high.

The order was given: if a firing solution presented itself, *Conqueror* was to attack.

**The Strike**

That afternoon, HMS *Conqueror* closed in. Commander Chris Wreford-Brown, her captain, faced the gravity of the moment. His submarine had stalked the cruiser for days. Now, with authorisation granted, he was prepared to fire. The weapon of choice was not the newer, more sophisticated Mark 24 Tigerfish torpedo, which had reliability issues, but the proven Mark 8—a Second World War-era design, unguided but devastating.

At 3:57 p.m., three torpedoes were launched. Two struck home. One slammed into *Belgrano*'s bow, ripping open compartments and killing dozens instantly. The second tore into her aft section near the engine room, destroying her power systems and sealing her fate. The third missed, running harmlessly on.

The effect was catastrophic. The ship shuddered under the impact, alarms blared, and lights flickered and died. Without power, pumps and communications systems failed. Flooding was rapid and uncontrollable. The cruiser, already ageing, had no chance against such wounds. Within minutes, she began to list heavily to port. Orders to abandon ship were given.

**Chaos on Deck**

For the crew, most of them young conscripts, the attack came without warning. One moment, they were carrying out routine duties in the cold Atlantic; the next, explosions ripped through the hull, plunging compartments into darkness and chaos. Sailors were thrown from their bunks, scalded by steam, or trapped by collapsing bulkheads. Some never made it out.

Those who did scrambled to the upper decks, donning lifejackets, searching for lifeboats, clinging to any hope of survival. Yet the ship was already tilting, making movement treacherous. Waves crashed over the rails, lifeboats jammed in their davits, and rafts had to be thrown directly into the sea. The water temperature hovered near freezing. Exposure could kill within minutes.

Accounts from survivors speak of terror, confusion, and extraordinary bravery. Officers tried to maintain order, shouting instructions over the roar of the wind and the groan of dying steel. Shipmates helped each other into rafts, pushed the injured toward safety, and prayed that rescue would come quickly.

Within twenty minutes of the first torpedo strike, the *Belgrano* rolled to port and slipped beneath the waves, her stern rising briefly before disappearing. A great bubble of air and oil erupted to the surface, marking the grave of the ship that had survived Pearl Harbour only to perish in the South Atlantic.

## The Human Cost

Three hundred twenty-three men perished—nearly half of Argentina's total casualties in the war. They were sons, brothers, fathers. Many were teenagers, conscripts serving their compulsory military duty. Their loss devastated families across Argentina. In towns and villages, news of the sinking spread with a mixture of grief and shock. Mothers wept, fathers raged, and communities mourned.

The survivors, numbering just over 700, endured hours in open rafts before rescue arrived. The Argentine Navy dispatched ships and helicopters, while civilian fishing vessels joined the desperate search. Survivors spoke of clinging to each other in the freezing water, singing songs to stay awake, and watching shipmates slip quietly into death from hypothermia. Rescues stretched into the following day. Many who had survived the initial sinking succumbed to exposure before help arrived.

## A Blow to Argentina

For the Argentine junta, the sinking was both a catastrophe and a rallying cry. Official statements framed the men as martyrs, heroes who had died defending the Malvinas. Yet behind the rhetoric lay bitter questions. Why had such an old and vulnerable ship been sent into harm's way? Could the deaths have been avoided?

Within the Navy, morale plummeted. The loss of *Belgrano* effectively ended Argentina's willingness to risk its surface fleet against the British task force. The navy withdrew to port, leaving the rest of the war to be fought mainly by aircraft and ground forces. Strategically, the sinking was decisive—it eliminated a significant threat and ensured British naval supremacy.

## Britain's View

In Britain, news of the sinking was greeted with relief in military circles. The Royal Navy had been handed a dangerous adversary in the form of *Belgrano* and her escorts. Her destruction removed a key element of Argentina's naval power. Admiral Sandy Woodward, commander of the task force, later admitted that as long as she remained at sea, he had feared for his carriers. After 2 May, that threat was gone.

Politically, however, the sinking sparked immediate controversy. Critics in Parliament and abroad noted that *Belgrano* had been outside the exclusion zone and appeared to be steaming away from the islands. Was her sinking, therefore, an act of self-defence or an unnecessary escalation? The government, led by Margaret Thatcher, defended the decision vigorously. The exclusion zone, they argued, was not a limit on British action but a warning to Argentina. Any hostile ship that threatened the task force, regardless of position, was a legitimate target.

In the House of Commons, Thatcher faced heated questions but stood firm. "The *Belgrano* was a danger to our boys," she declared. For her supporters, it was a necessary, even courageous, decision. For her opponents, it was an avoidable tragedy that hardened Argentina's resolve and complicated diplomatic efforts.

## The International Debate

Beyond Britain and Argentina, the sinking reverberated globally. In the United Nations, Argentina accused Britain of aggression, claiming the attack occurred during peace negotiations. Britain countered that the cruiser was part of a fleet manoeuvre and thus a legitimate target. Neutral observers were divided. Some saw it as a cold but necessary act of war; others condemned it as excessive.

Historians and legal scholars continue to debate the issue. Did the submarine strike fall within the laws of armed conflict? Was the exclusion zone binding or merely a warning? Could *Belgrano* have turned back to strike later had she been spared? These questions have ensured that her sinking remains one of the most studied naval engagements of the twentieth century.

## Memory and Mourning

For Argentina, the *Belgrano* became a national wound. Annual commemorations honour the sailors who died. Their names are etched into memorials, their sacrifice remembered as part of the country's struggle. For the families, the grief never entirely faded. Survivors, too, carried scars—physical and psychological. Many spoke of survivor's guilt, haunted by the faces of friends lost in the icy waters.

In Britain, the event entered public memory differently. For supporters of the war, it symbolised resolve—the willingness to act decisively to protect national interests. For critics, it epitomised the costs of war and the dangers of escalation. The debate resurfaced for years, shaping discussions of military ethics and government transparency.

## The End of a Long Journey

For the ship herself, the sinking marked the end of a remarkable career. From her launch in Camden in 1938 to her survival of Pearl Harbour, to her service in the Pacific, and finally to her rebirth as an Argentine symbol, she had lived two distinct lives. Her end was violent and tragic, but also historically resonant.

In her steel and rivets, she carried the ambitions of two nations. In her wake, she left stories of courage, sacrifice, and controversy. She was a witness to both the beginning and the end of global wars—born in the shadow of one, victorious in another, and destroyed in the Cold War's twilight. Few ships have lived such a complete and complex life.

## Chapter 10: Aftermath – Memory and Controversy

The story of the *General Belgrano* did not end on 2 May 1982 when she slipped beneath the icy waters of the South Atlantic. Her wreck may lie silent on the ocean floor, but her name, her crew, and the circumstances of her sinking continued to reverberate in both Argentina and Britain for decades. Few single events of the Falklands War have been so heavily scrutinised, mourned, politicised, and mythologised. For some, the sinking was a necessary military decision that removed a dangerous adversary. For others, it was an act of needless aggression, a tragedy that claimed the lives of hundreds of young men. Between these poles lies the complex reality of memory, politics, and history.

### Argentina's Wound

In Argentina, the loss of the cruiser was devastating. The 323 sailors who died represented nearly half of all Argentine casualties in the Falklands War. They were not abstract numbers but sons, brothers, husbands, and fathers. Many were teenage conscripts, barely out of school, pressed into service by the junta. Their average age was just nineteen. Entire towns and villages lost multiple young men, leaving communities shattered.

The Argentine government, facing defeat in the war and mounting unrest at home, sought to frame the *Belgrano* tragedy as a symbol of sacrifice. Official rhetoric portrayed the sailors as martyrs, men who had given their lives for the Malvinas cause. Annual commemorations were instituted. Streets, schools, and public squares were named in honour of the *Belgrano* and her crew. Monuments were erected, including a large memorial in Buenos Aires that lists the names of all who perished. For many families, these rituals of remembrance provided some measure of recognition, though they could not fill the absence left at dinner tables across the country.

Survivors played a vital role in keeping the memory alive. Their testimonies—of chaos, terror, and selfless acts of bravery during the ship's final minutes—became part of Argentina's collective consciousness. They spoke in schools, at public ceremonies, and in interviews, ensuring that the sacrifice of their comrades would not be forgotten. Yet their voices also carried pain. Survivors wrestled with trauma, guilt, and questions about why the ship had been sent into harm's way at all. Some publicly criticised the junta, blaming military leaders for reckless decisions that cost lives. Others struggled quietly, haunted by nightmares of cold water and the faces of shipmates lost to the sea.

**Britain's Debate**

Across the Atlantic, the event took on a different hue. For Britain, the sinking of the *Belgrano* was initially hailed as a military success. Admiral Sandy Woodward, commander of the task force, later admitted that the cruiser's presence had posed a significant threat. Her loss effectively neutralised the Argentine Navy as a surface force, allowing the British to concentrate on land operations and air defence. Strategically, the attack was decisive.

Yet politically, it soon became one of the war's most contentious issues. Within hours of the announcement, questions arose: why had the ship been attacked outside the Total Exclusion Zone? Had she been sailing away from the conflict rather than toward it? Was the sinking, therefore, necessary?

Prime Minister Margaret Thatcher faced heated debates in the House of Commons. Critics accused her of escalating the conflict, of deliberately targeting the *Belgrano* to harden Argentina's stance and undermine peace talks then underway in Peru. Supporters countered that exclusion zones were never meant to protect enemy warships—that any hostile vessel was a fair target. Thatcher herself remained unapologetic. Famously, when challenged in a BBC interview about the cruiser "sailing away," she shot back: "But it was a danger to our boys." That blunt phrase encapsulated her position: the ship's potential threat justified its destruction, regardless of its course or position.

The controversy persisted. Opposition MPs called for inquiries, demanding the release of classified documents. Over time, journalists and historians pieced together evidence, some of it contradictory, fuelling decades of debate. To Thatcher's admirers, her decision reflected resolve and courage in a time of war. To her detractors, it epitomised the ruthlessness and opacity of her government.

## International Reverberations

Beyond Argentina and Britain, the sinking reverberated internationally. Some governments condemned the attack, seeing it as excessive. Others viewed it as a legitimate act of war. The United Nations, already paralysed by divisions over the Falklands conflict, was unable to provide a definitive judgement.

Among naval analysts and military historians, the *Belgrano* case became a touchstone in discussions of exclusion zones, rules of engagement, and the laws of naval warfare. Could a declared exclusion zone implicitly restrict attacks beyond its boundary? Or did the principle of military necessity override such constraints? The case remains a staple in war colleges and legal debates, illustrating the grey areas of modern conflict.

## The Shipwreck as Symbol

The *Belgrano*'s wreck lies at a depth of more than 4,000 metres, southwest of the Falklands. It has never been disturbed, officially recognised as a war grave. For Argentina, it is sacred ground, a site of mourning comparable to a national cemetery. Families know their loved ones rest there, entombed within the steel hull.

From time to time, proposals have surfaced to locate or photograph the wreck with deep-sea technology. Such efforts are controversial. Some argue that documenting the site would honour the fallen, ensuring their resting place is not forgotten. Others fear it would be a violation of sacred memory, reducing a solemn grave to a spectacle. For now, the wreck remains undisturbed, hidden in darkness, a silent monument to the lives lost.

## Survivors and Families

The most powerful legacy lies with the survivors and the families of the fallen. In Argentina, groups such as the *Comisión de Familiares de Caídos en el Crucero ARA General Belgrano* continue to campaign for recognition and remembrance. Each year, on 2 May, ceremonies are held, wreaths are cast into the sea, and names are read aloud. For survivors, these gatherings are moments of solidarity but also reminders of trauma.

Many families never received bodies to bury. Their grief is bound to memory, photographs, and the rituals of commemoration. For some, the Argentine state's initial use of the tragedy as propaganda deepened their pain, feeling that their sons' lives were politicised rather than mourned. Over time, however, grassroots remembrance movements ensured that the sailors were honoured not as symbols but as individuals—ordinary young men caught in extraordinary events.

## The "What Ifs"

The sinking of the *Belgrano* is also remembered for the tantalising "what ifs." What if the submarine had not been ordered to fire? Would the cruiser have withdrawn harmlessly? Would she have turned back to strike? Could a negotiated peace, then being explored by Peru and the United States, have gained traction without the shock of the attack?

For historians, these questions are almost unanswerable, yet they fuel the enduring fascination with the event. For families, however, the counterfactuals are painful. To imagine a son or brother still alive had a single order not been given is to reopen wounds.

## A Divided Legacy

In the decades since 1982, the *General Belgrano* has come to symbolise different things to different people. In Argentina, she is remembered as a national tragedy, a reminder of the cost of authoritarian adventurism and the bravery of ordinary sailors. In Britain, she is both a symbol of naval power and a lightning rod in debates about Margaret Thatcher's leadership. In international law, she is a case study. In maritime tradition, she is one of the last large warships sunk by submarine torpedoes in wartime—a reminder that, even in the missile age, submarines could alter the course of conflict.

## Remembering the Ship That Lived Twice

It is striking to remember that this ship had already lived one whole life before the Falklands. As USS *Phoenix*, she had survived Pearl Harbour, fought across the Pacific, and steamed into Tokyo Bay at victory. To her American crew, she was a lucky ship. To her Argentine crew, she was a proud flagship. To history, she became the vessel that lived twice, only to die in the cold waters of the South Atlantic.

Her story is more than a footnote to the Falklands War. It is a thread that runs from the shipyards of New Jersey in the 1930s to the geopolitical struggles of the 1980s, from the Great Depression to the Cold War. Her legacy lies not only in steel and rivets but in memory—in the families who mourn, the politicians who argue, the historians who analyse, and the sailors who still remember the sound of the explosions and the chill of the sea.

## Conclusion

The sinking of the *General Belgrano* remains one of the most debated naval actions of the twentieth century. It was a moment where strategy, politics, and human cost collided in full view of the world. To study it is to grapple with questions that extend beyond the Falklands War: the limits of military necessity, the meaning of sacrifice, and the weight of political decisions that consign men to death.

The ship rests now in silence, but the debates above her resting place have never been stilled. For Argentina, she is a wound and a symbol. For Britain, she is a triumph shadowed by controversy. For the world, she is a reminder that warships, like the nations that sail them, carry within their hulls not only weapons but also stories of pride, tragedy, and the enduring struggle to make sense of conflict.

## Final Conclusion: The Ship That Lived Twice

From the moment her keel was laid at Camden, New Jersey, in the mid-1930s, the cruiser that would bear first the name USS *Phoenix* and later ARA *General Belgrano* was destined for an extraordinary path. She was born in an era of interwar uncertainty, when navies around the world balanced treaty restrictions with the looming shadow of another global conflict. She emerged sleek and bristling with firepower, part of the Brooklyn-class—a symbol of American industrial confidence at a time when much of the world was sliding into chaos. Her very name, *Phoenix*, was prophetic: a mythical bird reborn from flames, destined to endure fire and rise again.

The crucible of the Second World War shaped her first life. Moored at Pearl Harbour on 7 December 1941, she faced the Japanese attack that brought the United States into the conflict. Unlike so many of the proud battleships around her, she escaped the inferno, her guns blazing in defiance. From that day onward, she carried the imprint of survival. To her crew, she became a "lucky ship," and her luck would follow her through campaigns across the Pacific: supporting landings, bombarding enemy positions, screening carriers, and guarding the fragile arteries of supply.

For nearly four years, she was a constant presence in some of the Pacific's bloodiest campaigns, her decks shaken by the recoil of her nine six-inch guns, her sailors hardened by kamikaze raids and submarine threats. When Japan finally surrendered, the *Phoenix* steamed into Tokyo Bay, part of the Allied armada that bore witness to the end of the most devastating war in human history. She had travelled the whole arc from Pearl Harbour to victory. For her American crew, she was not merely a warship but a home, a companion, and ultimately a veteran in steel of a war that reshaped the world order.

Yet peace is rarely kind to fleets built for war. By the 1950s, the United States no longer needed the vast armada that had carried it to victory. Dozens of cruisers were scrapped or mothballed. But the *Phoenix* was not to be consigned to oblivion. Instead, she was transferred to a new home, purchased by Argentina and rechristened *General Belgrano* in honour of a founding father of Argentine independence. Thus began her second life.

In Argentina, she was more than just an addition to the navy. She was a statement: a declaration that the nation aspired to regional leadership and international recognition. Crewed by a new generation of sailors, many of whom knew little of her American past, she became a floating symbol of Argentine pride and ambition. She represented prestige in Latin America, a vessel that could show the flag abroad, host presidents, and remind neighbours that Argentina remained a maritime power. For the men who trained on her decks, she was not an ageing second-hand cruiser but a proud flagship.

Through the 1950s, 60s, and 70s, *Belgrano* embodied both continuity and contradiction. She was at once a formidable warship by South American standards and a relic in a world where missiles, jets, and nuclear submarines were redefining naval warfare. Yet symbols often matter as much as capabilities. For Argentina's leaders, the sight of *Belgrano* cutting through southern seas or appearing in foreign harbours was a projection of power and legitimacy. She was an ambassador as much as a war machine.

Her second life reached its tragic climax in 1982. When Argentina's military junta launched its ill-fated seizure of the Falkland Islands, *Belgrano* was drawn once more into front-line service. Despite her age, she sailed south with pride, her young crew operating the same guns that had thundered in the Pacific four decades earlier. She entered the South Atlantic as both symbol and threat—an anachronism perhaps, yet still a warship with the power to alter the balance. On 2 May, her fate was sealed when HMS *Conqueror*, a British nuclear submarine, launched the torpedoes that sent her to the bottom.

The sinking claimed 323 Argentine lives—nearly half the nation's total casualties in the Falklands War. It silenced the *Belgrano* forever, but it also ensured her place in history. Overnight, she became one of the most famous ships of the twentieth century, her loss sparking debate in parliaments, protests on streets, and memorials on both sides of the Atlantic.

For Argentina, the *Belgrano* became a national wound. Entire towns were left grieving; families received no bodies to bury, only the knowledge that their loved ones rested in the cold dark of the South Atlantic. To this day, ceremonies are held annually, wreaths are cast into the sea, and names are read aloud. She is remembered as a symbol of sacrifice, the sailors as martyrs to the Malvinas cause, and the ship herself as a vessel of honour.

For Britain, the sinking was both a triumph and a controversy. Militarily, it neutralised a significant threat to the task force. Politically, it became one of Margaret Thatcher's defining moments, hailed by some as a display of resolve and condemned by others as unnecessary and reckless. Internationally, the sinking became a touchstone for debates about the laws of war, the legitimacy of exclusion zones, and the ethics of submarine warfare. Historians still pore over charts and orders, asking whether the cruiser was sailing toward or away from the combat zone when the fatal decision was made.

The *Belgrano*'s legacy, then, is multifaceted. She is remembered as a veteran of Pearl Harbour and the Pacific, as Argentina's proud flagship, as a casualty of the Falklands, and as a case study in the dilemmas of modern warfare. Few warships have lived such complex, layered lives.

Yet beyond strategy and symbolism lies the human dimension. The ship was nothing without the sailors who walked her decks. They were Americans in the 1940s, fighting to end fascism. They were Argentines in the 1980s, caught in the ambitions of a junta. They were teenagers learning discipline, veterans recalling camaraderie, officers shouldering responsibility. To remember the *Phoenix/Belgrano* is to place them: their courage, their laughter, their fear, and their sacrifice.

Her name—first the *Phoenix*, then the *Belgrano*—reminds us of resilience and tragedy. She was forged in one war, survived another, and perished in a third. She linked continents and generations, embodying both the endurance of steel and the fragility of human life. She remains a ship that lived twice, and in doing so, reflected the turbulent century she sailed through.

To study her history is not merely to catalogue naval architecture or battle reports. It is to confront the great themes of the twentieth century: the industrial might of nations, the ambitions of leaders, the devastation of global war, the uncertainties of the Cold War, and the human cost of conflict. Her story begins with rivets hammered in a New Jersey shipyard and ends in the silence of the South Atlantic seabed. Between those two points lies a narrative of survival, pride, controversy, and loss.

And so, the conclusion of her story is not an ending at all but an invitation: to remember, to reflect, and to recognise that behind every ship's name lies the echo of lives lived and lost. The USS *Phoenix* and ARA *General Belgrano* were the same vessel, but they carried the dreams and grief of two nations. Their story is a microcosm of history itself—an account of resilience, transformation, and tragedy on the high seas.

This has been a Zentara UK production. For more information, search for 'Zentara UK' on Audible and Amazon.

9 798265 725257